Mystical Poetry

Deborah Morrison

Canadian Cataloguing in Publication Data:

Morrison, Deborah
Mystical Poetry
ISBN 0-9685803-1-9
    1. Mysticism—Poetry. I. Title.

PS8576.07413M98 2000   C811'.6   COO-01619-8
PR9199.3.M65233M98 2000

Copyright 2000 by Deborah Morrison.
Published Oct. 2000 by Manor House Publishing

Manor House Publishing Inc.
(905) 648-2193

Foreword

It's a rare and privileged moment when any work of writing immediately captivates your imagination and touches your soul.

Deborah Morrison's Mystical Poetry has just such a commanding impact on your senses, your thoughts, your state of being.

To read this inspiring collection of poems is to become moved and enthralled by timeless messages of peace, love, non-violence and appreciation for those we hold dear.

Deborah Morrison conveys and imbues her thoughts with a potent combination of mysticism and sensuality. Each poem transcends time and space and memory, allowing the reader to interpret her messages and imagery in purely personal terms.

Mystical Poetry is waiting to take you on a journey of self discovery, love and mysticism.
It's a journey well worth taking. And so it begins.

- **Michael B. Davie,**
    Author, Inside The Witches' Coven.

About the author

Deborah Morrison is a Hamilton poet/writer who draws inspiration from the Steel City, nature, people and Far Eastern mysticism.

She's also a psychotherapist/counsellor, early childhood educator and yoga instructor.

Deborah Morrison holds an Honours Degree in Religious Studies/Sociology and has extensively researched Eastern and Western thought in the context of contemporary and comparative studies, non-violence and mysticism.

She's taken a holistic approach to writing, teaching, meditation, stress management, early childhood education, psychotherapy, yoga and counselling for over 20 years.

Deborah Morrison has also written several articles on natural and homeopathic medicine, yoga, psychology and metaphysics.

She is a distinguished member of the International Society of Poetry and has had numerous poems published through the International Library of Poetry.

Manor House Publishing is proud to bring this important Canadian writer's work to a growing and appreciative audience.

Mystical Poetry is her first book of poems.

Introduction:
A Mystical Journey

Mystical experience encompasses a consciousness that eternally goes beyond, from one Truth to the next.

Furthermore, mysticism can be understood in relation to non-violence, as embracing the concept of joy, and in terms of its practical application in face of social tension.

There are various dimensions of mysticism; and all dimensions ultimately converge at a point that is theocentric at heart!

One dimension is service encompassing self-sacrifice and self-purification that leads one to the enlightenment of direct mystical experience.

To live one's life based on simplicity, non-violence, and Truth is the practical, day to day application of mystical vision.

Everyone has the potential and ability to live the mystical life! With this in mind, mysticism may be termed spirituality in action. Moreover, mysticism is synonymous with spiritual power or Gnostic energy.

Such spiritual power is simultaneously all pervasive and immanent in our entire existence past, present and future.

Transcend the ego and awaken to the wonders of mystical experience.

Mysticism is the essence of the human soul, and suggests a return to the roots of our consciousness. Thereby mystical experience enhances one's capacity for higher feeling.

By means of Love (not hatred) one abides in the power to see inwardly and in fullness. Esoterically, the mystic melts into Love, and Love melts into the mystic!

At a practical level, mysticism approaches life in terms of non-violence; action based on the decision to never harm deliberately.

Another practical dimension of mysticism is that materialism can be transformed in the vision of spiritual harmony.

With non-violence the spirit can transform matter by means of the Soul-force generated. Essentially mysticism aims at a philosophy and practice based on non-violent action.

Furthermore, mystical experience takes one on an inward journey into one's own consciousness. This inner journey enables one to become more fully self-aware.

What is remarkable in mysticism is the flowering of the pursuit of the benevolence of humankind, as a means toward enhancement of mystic fulfilment. One begins the journey inwardly by the process of inward vision.

However, one continues the journey through the observance of outward activities based on non-violence, simplicity and Truth.

Always affirm goodness to all living beings. Non-violence is the means to embrace the mystical vision of Truth, peace and Love.

The modern social pattern of utilitarianism necessitates a mystical, joyous breakthrough! Much of the modern world is devoid of mutual co-operation, cohesion and sincere,
compassionate feeling for one and all.

Mystical experience heightens one's capacity for Love. Love is the remedy for all suffering of distressed humanity.

Discover the mystical concept of joy that reflects the conscious awareness of brilliant radiance Divine!

Mystically embrace all creation as the eternal life-stream of joy. Free the Self to live the mystical life with true devotion and a pure heart! This book about exploring mysticism and appreciating its relevance in our lives.

With poetry and peace,
- **Deborah Morrison**

DEDICATION

I lovingly dedicate this book to my children Jared, Brandon and Leah-Rose.

My sincere thanks as well to the following inspirational people: Joan Henshaw (mother), Rabbi Irwin Zeplowitz and the Minyonaires, Reverend Jane Drotar, Nettie Snaddon, Rita Harrison, Tracey Munro, Nicole Carson, Dr. Marilyn May, Madeline Zeldin, Ron Marinelli, Jim Miner, Katie and Bob Hebert, Eleanore and Richard Kosydar, Linda Quinn, Robyn McInnis, Joseph Waxman, Karen Orgel, Brian Fisher, Rita Harrison, Richard Green, Elizabeth Dalgleish, Arvind Singh and Swami Vishnudevananda.

I also extend profound, sincere regards to the memory of Denise Capponi.

Thanks also to editor Michael B. Davie and Manor House Publishing for bringing this first book of poetry from dream to reality.

Finally, my thanks to all others, too numerous to mention, who have helped me succeed.

- Deborah Morrison

ETERNAL PLAYMATE

Dissolved into ecstasies
Overwhelmed with Divine emotions
Teasing and playing
Self-forgetful
A spontaneous transcendence emerges
Our eyes sparkling
With inner joy
The essence of Love
Enfolds us
And so loveliness blossoms
Anew in Your presence
Within one another
The nectar of Love
Overflows
I am tempted
To taste it eternally
My only desire
Is to be ever in your embrace

ONE

I delight
In the service
Of your
Every desire

Raise me in
Your arms
Hold me
Close to your
Heart

I was crying
In the dark
And now
With you
Joy is overflowing
You are my all,
I have found
In you
My every need
You are the
Fulfilment
Of my heart's
Desire, I surrender
My self to you
In your embrace
I forget all else, as

A shimmering
Of auspicious colour
Enfolds my body and soul
With an aura
Of loveliness we
Two are one,
Enlightened in love
Every aspect of
My being is sweetened
With the honey
Of your charms
I revel and dance
In the measureless
Expression
Of our shared affection

You are my heaven
The destiny of my soul,
In my adoration of you

A pure golden flame
Of divine brilliance
Shines forth

My only fear now
Is lest
In some way
I may fail
To please you
And yet somehow
I know well

That even then
Our love would be
Changeless and infinite, I trust that
Never again can
We lose one another

I rejoice that
Through grace and kindness
We have found ourselves
As soul mates, now
And for eternity

My heart is simply
Saturated with love
I can no longer
Even for a second
Think of anything
But you,
My Beloved

FLAME

The all-embracing grasp,
Our soulful love…
One…
Manifest power, circulating energy
Conjoint souls are we,
Entwined in Divine play of
Amorousness, I adore you…
Enamoured by the very memory
Of your touch, Longing for the fullness of
you,
Quiescence enfolds
The spheres of my being, yet a teardrop falls
And yet I am set ablaze, I wait for you,
To be both one and the other
Renewal…
Light my heart
With your flame
Angel-star
Whisper softly, let my heart take wing
Play our love game again and again
Ecstasy…

SACRED LOTUS

Convergence
Human and Divine
Dialectics of desire
Heart within
The heart
Co-creativity
Essence of the
Infinite centre
Mystery of the
Timeless moment
When the sacred lotus blooms
To fullness
Each petal
Reflects the golden
Luminescence
And so to union Divine
By means of a spiritual walk
Along a pathway of peace,
...Non-violence...
Truth of being, Life-stream
Converges as compassion
Gracefully awakens the inner voice
And the integral response, the revelation
Of rapture
Heart, mind, body, spirit, and
Soulful life-purpose
At last guides one to
Enlightenment
Sacred lotus

Even as a seed
You are beautiful
In potentiality
Sacred lotus
Even in the earthbound darkness
You sprout life anew
And as a tiny bud
You are so very precious
To the entire cosmos
And even more precious
To me
Sacred lotus
In full bloom
You are my inspiration,
Fragrance of flower,
Adorned with
The waters chinquapin
Sacred lotus
Your life purpose
Adrift, liminal
In the threshold
Between muddy earthen depths
And ethereal starlit skies
Sacred lotus
Free and elegant, afloat
On the waters of life…
And as a celestial navigator
You are my guide to true home,
As we journey together
From emergence toward original
Convergence

INTO LOVE EVERLASTING

Upon this sleepy healing planet
The children of the One awaken
Responding to light
And love of all
Seeing
For the first time
The many realities,
A tapestry of synchronicity…
Uncovering answers
It is now the "time"
That has been so deemed
By the One
Shadows dissolve in the light
Of Truth
Stirrings of memories, visions…
Cascades of
Words, overflowing,
Like cosmic wisdom
Throughout the universes of
Simultaneous experience, joyously
The enlightened children
Ascend in spiritual progression
Afforded insight
And knowing
On different realms of spiritual existence
To focus on this awareness
Of the sacred moment
While still in their bodies
Of flesh and blood

Not in the future
As a vision
Or in the past
As a memory
But in the now
In a moment
When the NOW is
Precise with
Higher knowing, incorporated
Wondrously in an ascension progression…
The enlightened children
Have received, and set into motion
Their needed energy
On a holistic scale
Involving all brothers and sisters,
Now is the "time"
To deliver what is needed
To assist in lucid perception
Of light all around
Why endure such earthly "sufferings"
From isolation, disease, hatred, war,
To avarice, jealousy, poverty, pain,
Climactic upheavals and ignorance?
In our pure love for the Divine Eternal One
We yearned for the closest
Bond that has been set
Into motion in existence
The Eternal One
Has dreamed creatively…
 "To experience separation
To know complete union"

With the agreement that
We would return
Each one has made
The promise
To return
To the Eternal One
This earthly existence
In the flesh
Is to experience Total Oneness
With the promise to
Return home
To the Divine Eternal One
To return "Home"
When the body
No longer functions
On this planet.
All who come here
Have made this promise,
There is a Divine space
Where all creation began
Where all come into
Completed form
As a perfect thought
Once set into motion
The many universes
Came into being
Simultaneously
As did each one of us,
With identity and life purpose
One devotion
Multifaceted and perfect

Each with a personal concept
And instant knowing of where to fit in, The first
"choice"
Truly a yearning of the spirit
An individualized life purpose
A desire for oneness
Completion of oneself
Healers, planners, builders,
Poets, teachers, prophets,
Artists, musicians and
Soul mates
Why have I not remembered?
Since the spiritual
Is overshadowed simply
By the condition
Of this three dimensional world
True Self
Begins the task
Of bringing forth
The remembering of
Our knowing
…Your identity…
…Your choice of devotion…
Since all time
Is simultaneous

Look in
While asleep and
Spiritually awaken
The enlightened children can "see"
Even when awake,

Remember the specifics
Of your individual mission
And of your unified mission
Each one
With conscious
Understanding
Of how to use those
Skills on earth
Call on intuition
Keep focused in the light
And on the Divine Eternal One

The loving purpose
Will move us forward
Re-ascend
Relinquish the magnetic pull
To the physical experience
And it shall begin
There is no need to be overwhelmed
For there is more help
Now than ever

Just ask
And it shall be there,
Such a great adventure
Into everlasting
Love everlasting

MORE THAN A MOMENT'S RAPTURE

His charm
Would have depth, mystery
Inspiration for me
In the moments following
His voice
More than an instant of
Rapture
His essence obscure, numinous
As if a decree from the Divine
His presiding power, his spirit
At play with my soul
Was luminescence,
Lightning,
The thunder of Jupiter
His closeness
As the distance between us
Was set free
Enabled me to glimpse
The eternal that was hidden
Behind the surfaces of the temporal
The essence of enchantment,
More than a moment's rapture
When I suddenly realized
That the spirit of his voice
Whispered
To the soul of my heart,
The dialectic of the sacred
Was Revealing and hiding, mystical…
Therein was the truth

CREATIVE SPIRITUALITY

Creation
Verging on the Mystical
Existence loved for its own sake
Being...Being...Being...
The glory of Existence
Creative spirituality happening
Doing...Doing...Doing...
A certain Divinity exists in
Everything in Everyone
In all that is
All that flows
From the Divine Source, creative energy
A light that shines in the dark
A light that darkness cannot overpower
The True Light
That Enlightens One and all
Active, imaginative, playful,
Ever Flowing
Unfolding, the Divine Creation is as ongoing
As we are in the innermost realms of the Soul
Full of Grace
Of Truth
Of creative spirituality,
And ecstatic with heaven
That is set ablaze within,
Becomes manifest as mystical experience
as creativity
That reveals magnificent treasures
Beyond our imaginings

APOLOGIES OF LOVE

I thought love could be controlled
It cannot
I thought love would adapt to me
It does not
Needs, expectations, societal
Coerce—
Obscurity of grey cloud
Cast in the azure of a warm summer sky
…Through silences…
Between the spoken word
Illuminates all that is done
Manifest reality, acts and intentions
Seen in a new light
Deeds of omission and commission
All that is nearest now
Contrasts become defined
A whisper of emergence
Is yet unnoticed
All rests on a contingency
Of the superstructure
Of what is "supposed to be"
Are we really loving yet?
Emulating even an insignificant degree of Truth?
An appropriate future should form
Should it not?
A process even though "slightly"
A compromise Of heart's desire, an apology
Heart shattering, but nevertheless prolific
A do not disturb or disrupt policy is well maintained

And the distance kept and enforced
Is so utterly "acceptable"
Submissions of nebulous order
Versus
The spontaneity of authenticity
Perspicacious
Yet paradoxically
Corrosive and carcinogenic, in a spiritual sense
In essence
A soul fragmented
But invisibly so
Besides the visual effects
Are purely "natural",
The flower
Merely blossoms then falls
To die, isn't it "supposed" to be so?
The historicity of the flower
Has a linear natural pattern
To display, each one is an experience, unique, "progressive"
The rhythms of time, the "beauty" of it.
The flower once had
Petals profuse, dynamic
Prolific
As they intertwined
Into an abundance, a forever One,
Splendour blossoms
With the transcendence of eternity
The beauty was brief, but wasn't the depth profound?
As the quest toward mundane success surfaces
Apparently, deliberately, it

Severed the blossom from where it had been
The fall was swift, silent
"Natural" yet also
Final. Was it spiritual? Logically
Argued that it is natural and therefore to be
Accepted with grace
As grace
All I do now is wonder what kind of grace
Imposition or Divine?
Can the dew of Heaven bless this union now?
The nectar of Divine will is sublime,
Devotion, pure and lovely
Yet the waters separate from the sky
In the horizon, Just look into the distance.
My hand trembles before such a "destiny"
Or perhaps before such a "tragic comedy."
To think that love could be controlled.
The best part of love does not answer
To any conscious intent
Can you see it too?
Or is it just a peculiarity of perception?
Nevertheless
I hope and pray that you will accept
My most humble and sincere
Apologies
Of
Love.

SONG

This Eternal Divine Music
Permeates One and All
I hear its harmonies
In my dreams
I see its melodies
Reflected in each and every twinkling moment
I feel its silent presence
Resounding in the depths of my soul
Silent essence, a
Melodious symphony
I smell it in the cascade of aromatics
So free in fields
Of wildflower
I taste it
The honey of nature's bounty
The sweetness of love
Life plays
Like a beautiful hymn
A sacred symphony of
One Being
My consciousness merges into the very silence
Of its sound
Transformed
Losing all sense of my separate existence
Effacing ego
I let in Divinity
Which already exists
Within
A splendour of expressive effulgence
Spiritual life
Eternal song
Reverberating throughout the

Cosmos
Reflected in my heart
The heights of Spirit
The depths of Soul
Spark
Of Divine Light
Is set ablaze
Forever and every
Rhythm
Of this Song of Silence
Chants its sweet song
To its mate
I hear the silver bells
Awakening of twinkling stars Melodies of
Ocean's spirit
The golden flute resounds
Its' never ending song
The sound springs melodiously
From the essence of the
One
The be-all and end-all
Echoing and re-echoing
Love
And rings
True
I need only silence myself
Look deep into your eyes
 And then I hear it all over
Again
Then the ears of my soul
At the threshold of my heart
Hear a wondrous symphony
From the Heavens
Above all the skies

HUMILITY

Non-assertion of egoism, humility
Is the way
That helps in knowing
Divine Will, look within
As the Soul ascends
Into higher spiritual planes
From possibility to possibility
Understand the mystery of Self
And the universe, and always
Follow your star...
Pure spirit reigns supreme,
Everlasting joy and peace,
Rise into Universal Mind
Meditate and discover
Priceless jewels of Divinity,
Enjoy the incessant Bliss
Of perpetual joy
And Supreme Happiness

BLESSING

True Blessing
Is a pure heart
The key
That unlocks the door
Leading to the mansions
Of the Cosmos
Be patient
Practice Equanimity
Of Mind
Listen to the silence
And Be
In union with The Divine
Love
With such intensity and
Be free
To proceed with Grace
Give freely to all
According to the need
Of each
Follow spirit
With true dedication
Work as a humble servant
Unostentatious service, know that
All is received from the Divine
And all is humbly given to the Divine
Drink the Supreme nectar
Of transcending all divisions
Perceive the All within "One" self and
Peacefully abide

RELIGION AND SPIRITUALITY

Organized religion
Prayers
Of set phrases
Forced ceremonials
Time-consuming rituals
Adherence to
Outward symbols
At the sacrifice
Of their inner spiritual meaning
Superiority of one creed
Over another, Power plays
Of one religion waging war
Against another
Spiritual brothers and sisters
Fighting with each other
Because there are differences of opinion
About what is the Truth
War, falsehood, hatred, and intolerance
Often preached in the name of religion
With the honour of God
And the compassionate service of
Humanity
Set aside

Love has vanished altogether
Reducing religion
To a mere profession of creeds and dogmas
A "profitable" mega-business

Words replace deeds
Religion, no longer concerned with
Knowledge of one's Self
And union with Divine origin
They seek God in the observance
Of outward means
Repetition of verbal formula
Pilgrimages, Temples, Churches,
Amidst unfeeling hearts
Reveal the depths to which
Religion may descend
Many God-gifted ones of the past
Have turned away from
Fossilized religion
And ritualistically encoded "Truth"
It is a sorrowful spectacle
And I ask
"Where is love? Where is Truth?"

Slavery is not the aim of religion
Not to bind, but to set humanity
Free from its slavery
Nature does not distinguish
Between one's race or religion
All belong to one humanity on earth
All are equal

Together
We learn the same lessons
From the only true teacher
Universal Cosmos

Where no distinctions are observed
Such is the true essence of Spirituality
Care for One and All
Love each other and
Learn that all faiths are to be
Respected
From the perspective that
There is no religion without a
Spark of Truth in it
The essence of Spirituality
Is radiant throughout
The teachings of all the
Great Scriptures

The Master-Souls teach
There is One Being
One Divine Light of Truth
That guides humanity
Such is spirituality
The quintessential reality
Of Love and Truth
Of compassion
And I know that
"Here" is Love, here…
Where the sound of Silence is heard
And the Soul is carried across
This Ocean of nescience
At-One-ment
Such
Is
Love, Truth

STAR BLANKET

Give it all away
But be careful
The ego will take the form of pride
This is worse than the pride of wealth
People will admire
Such a spirit of renunciation
You may become famous
And the pride of wealth
Will return by and by...
The ego is ever ready
To assume new forms
Sometime wondrous
Sometimes fallen
Sometimes subtle
But always dangerous
There is a great power
Realize Akarta
I am non-doer
Realize Abhoktha
I am non-enjoyer
Realize Sakshi
I am a witness
Forbearance is the touchstone
To bear insult and injury
This is our highest Sadhana
To walk the talk
Our spiritual practice...
And in so doing
Ascertain the extent
To which the inner personality
Has been purified by
Reflection...

Live, work, and love
Not because there is anything to gain
But because it is Divine Will
Designed to promote the wellness of
All Being...
Even with ill health and financial break-down
Our precious life has been prolonged
To do the Divine Will
Fortune smiles intermittently
A transient joy to behold...
Surrender
Cease not from delivering
The message of Divine Life
Our foremost duty...
To serve...
And whatever service is rendered
Is quickly consumed
 in the Divine Fire
Of Akarta-Abokta-Bhavana
Prosperity and adversity
Spins 'round our days
Our hearts...
Journey on
Indifferent to honour and dishonour
Pain and pleasure
Gain and loss
Love spins 'round our hearts
With tears of joy and sorrow
But be careful lest the ego take form
Upon form, in its recurrent quest
For sense gratification
Give it all away, surrender...
Spin stars
upon the blanket of our Soul

ASPECTS OF BEING
(for Brandon)

Enchantment enlightens my days
As I walk a winding path
That follows my intuitions
My vision is seen passionately, as love,
Even with eyes of sacred seeing
A visionary quest
I hear, oh song of my soul
Resounding elegantly, as true
In the fullness of silence
Faithfully I dance along
To the music of
My inspirations
With the aromatic sweetness
Of my dream, revealing richness to
Every aspect of my being
My eyes reflect a wealth of possibilities
As I discover deeper meaning
In each step along
The Way
Healing and renewal
Spring forth, energizing aspects of Being
As I discover, one sacred space
One sacred place
And then another, and another…
The destination remains a mystery,
Yet with passion and vision
I creatively journey on

WHAT THEN MY LOVE?

Rare sensations
Awesome
Glimpses of the Eternal
Hidden
Behind the temporal

Our love
Like an ancient
Earthen pot of clay
Full of cracks

Like a house of old
Full of windows and
Doorways, incongruent and

Bent, not perfectly square

Our life together
Was full of cracks,
Nevertheless, my love,
Was that not where the
Unexpectedly numinous
Momentarily did appear?
What then, my love?

EVERYTHING FLOWS

The heart of imagination stirs
Deepening, ever deepening…
Soul seeks roots
Spirit desires wings
Tension arises,
Wherein the Divine sparks,
Connect
The Heavens unto the Earth
Shape, time and space
Enhance the heart…
And know that you can
Never step into
The same waters twice

MIND SO FREE
(for Jared)

Most beautiful to see
A mind so free…
Free from the least trace
Of narrowness
And worldly wisdom
Like a shooting star
Exuberance of action
Reflected at every step
Spontaneous artfulness and
Philosophic depth of mind
A wondrous blend of
Sage and child
Open-hearted with
Serene confidence and
Equanimity
Seeing all with
Freedom and equality
Supreme calmness pervades
Body, mind, heart, spirit and soul
Having found the centre
And ever living in it
Unruffled by emotion or circumstance
And at all times
Being
Serenity personified
So sweet and gentle
Most beautiful to see
A mind so free…

EXPANSION OF THE HEART

True expansion of the heart
Is very, very rare and
The quick and ready
Impulse to give
Does not come easily to everyone

Large-hearted liberality
...Take everything and
Give to the other...
Then as real power
Blossoms into equanimity
A great dignity will radiate
Self-confidence
Quiet strength
Coupled with the force
Of a glance that is
Felt immediately,
Doubtless the direct outcome
Of a most merciful melting
Be content
Reduce your wants
And ever share
What you have with others

PRACTISE LOVE

Never harm
Anyone
Non-injury
Is the highest virtue
Develop high thinking
Lead a happy, simple
Contented life
Be detached
Have forgiveness and be
Compassionate

"SELF" RELIANT

Abide in Eternity and Infinity
Oh Immortal Self, so True
Do not be dependant upon…
Abide in "Self" reliance
The highest of all virtues
Remember the Divine
Virtuous qualities
Of strength, power
As the key to peace
This is the essence
Of Spirituality

TIMELESS

Life is brief
Time is fleeting
Arise
Awake
And realize the
Self

DO IT NOW

Time and tide are most precious
They are two mighty forces
That never come back
Neither to be held up
Or called back
For the convenience
Of anyone
Odd bits of time slip away
Unnoticed by anyone
Waste not
One hour
Set with sixty diamond minutes
Oh single moment
As priceless as a jewel…
Now is later than you think!

THE DIFFERENCE

There exists the difference
Between the mere "saying"
Of certain things and
Actually "Being" and "Doing" them
Oneself

People are not generally
Moved to action
By the words of a person
But almost unconsciously and
Inspirationally
By observing actual
Living precepts
Actually live
Exhortations uttered to
Evoke emulation,
This is the modern
Miracle…
The utter sincerity
Of one's life
Exacting correspondence
Of life actualized to

Beliefs upheld
Constantly endeavour
To embody in life
Whatever is spoken or written

BELOVED ROSE
(for Leah-Rose)

You come into my life
And teach me how to see
You share your soul
With mine, now and eternally
You stay so very near
Lifting my fear when I was down
You come into my life
And teach me how to see...
You give both truth and love
And with compassion cherish me
I look into your eyes
Selfless, pure and peacefully,
Once all was black and white
Now radiant light with darkness gone
You bring colour to me now
From midnight until dawn...
My sunrise glistens now with gold
My sunset violet shades behold
The roses painted red with silver dew
My daybreak skies now azure blue
The leaves are emerald with rich green...
My life of black and white unseen,
Because you come into my life
And teach me how to see

LIMINAL SPHERE

In a sphere
That's neither
Here nor there
One is at the threshold
Neither inside or out
Rather somewhere
In between
Here or there
Is not befitting
Of where one's
Self is now
Moved on from here
And having not yet reached there,
Within a sphere of the liminal
Replete with wonder
Abundant with inner stirrings
Hopes, dreams, and visions
The threshold experience
Elucidated by design
Further expressed by
Space, symmetry, unity and
Movement in one's life
As some prominent
Elements of form,
Is a "place" or
Inner state of being
A liminal zone, threshold space
A place that is
Neither here nor there

Typically symbolic
Of a turning point
Or a change in consciousness,
One appears to be "still"...
Paradoxically
There is great activity
On the inner level of one's being,
And as a result one experiences
A transformation from "here" to "there"
Literally, or perhaps on the metaphysical
Level
Dusk, twilight
The moments between waking
And sleep
Are liminal zones, threshold experiences,
Imagine the central focus as an
Entrance to the garden,
Open French doors,
Framing an empty wicker chair
Emptiness...
That overlooks the garden,
This is the threshold space
A secondary focus of activity surfaces
As a response to the stillness,
A response to the threshold experience
Of the primary focus,
The activity is of the nature of
Harmony, creativity, inner peace
Even while doing daily activities,
A bringing one back to one's
Centre of peace

And stillness
By means of the liminal
A "composition" is created
That is generally symmetrical
By use of colour, line, and form,
Colour in muted tones
The nuance of hue is suggestive
Of a mood of tranquility
The lines are
Soft, flowing, graceful,
The lines at the entrance
Are in contrast straight and angular
This contrast suggests
The primary importance of
The unassuming, gentle
Threshold space of
Forms that blend into one another
Creating balance and the
Liminal sphere of
Direct mystical experience

WONDROUS TO BEHOLD

Direct expression
Of spiritually oriented
Themes can be achieved
Only within the
Confines
Of a chosen
Paradigmatic framework,
Indirect expression affords
More room
For creativity
Inspiration
But the essence
Must be hinted at
Carefully veiled
In metaphor, symbolism
Analogies, parables
Any aspect of Truth
Even hinted at
Resonates with
One's Higher Self
The mists are
Wondrous and beautiful
Since they maintain
An aspect of mystery
The indirect
Wonder, unformed, still becoming
While creatively veiling "the clearing"
That emerges as clearly delineated
Form Truth Absolute

GEMS OF WISDOM

Oh diamond
Lightening bolt
Beloved of Venus,
Oh scarlet
Ruby, garnet
Red jewel
Your are a
Red-lotus coloured jewel
Gem of the sun,
Oh wondrous
Pearl
Falling star
You are the gem of mind
Jewel of moon,
Oh brilliant
Yellow sapphire
Beloved of Jupiter
Orange jewel
King of flowers,
Oh sparkling
Hessonite
Orange gem of the moon
Reflecting of genius,
Oh emerald
Communication, clairvoyance
Charm of good fortune,
Oh azure
Blue, sapphire
Saturn's gem

Blue
Royal blue gem,
Oh mystic ochre
Coral
The coral tree
Gem of Mars
Being soul of the ocean,
Oh pure
Jade
Translucent
Intense pure green

Free me of past
Misfortune,
Oh transparent
Quartz
Rock crystal
Gem removing fear
Crystal jewel,
Oh moonstone
Moon of the earth
Beloved of the moon,
Show me the way to
The jewel of love
Oh gems
Of wisdom
Mystic virtue
Guides of beauty and
Truth

SACRED CIRCLE

Why does the snowflake melt?
To enliven spring flowers,
Why does summer sun blaze?
To ripen the garden,
Why does the leaf fall?
To bring forth beautiful snow...
Why do the seasons dance so?
To embrace us in the sacred circle

DIVINE ESSENCE

The Divine essence
Is within all of us
We cannot package the
Divine in a box...
To catch a full glimpse of the Divine
All around us,
Contained within and without...
Realize on the transcendental plane
 That the Divine is formless,
 In that all forms represent the
Manifestation of the Divine Spirit,
Yet none of them can claim to have
The fullness of the Infinite...
Countless universal manifestations
Exist of the unmanifest,
And the paths to the sacred
Are Limitless...

SPIRITUAL MYSTERY

Upward soaring
Being
Rise
Away from
Materiality, ego, disharmony

Uplift
Guide
Toward
A personal
Inner experience Divine

Propel the stars
Synchronize
The vast, intricate
Dance
Of the cosmos

Guardian
Of body and soul
What's impossible
May be possible
Through
Your sacred service

Behold
Your body assumed
A guise
For engaging in

Earthly ministry
Transcend
The boundaries of
Time, space and matter
As mystic celestial
You are Love
Incarnate

Share
Light
With those on a
Long journey
To recover heart and
Soul

Shining being
Of venerable aspect

With compassion and
Insight
Your spiritual eyes
Reveal the
Truth
That Life
Is Love
And Love
Is
Life

THE COSMIC DANCE

Very ancient, the Cosmic Dance
Auspicious and benevolent
Simultaneously destructive and sanguinary
For destruction cannot be separated
From creation
The opposite poles cannot exist without the other
Paradoxical, however in reality a bipolar synthesis
The two contradictory concepts commingle
And form an integral concept
As the attributes of destruction are collected
Into the universal whole of creation
One reality, transcendent yet conceived
In many forms, as a coin has two faces
Likewise the Divine has three known phases;
Creator, Maintainer, Destroyer
Creation and dissolution take place each moment
And constitute the Cosmic Dance
The "Eternal" is the universal dancer
Whose dancing creates the outflow and in flow
Of the universes, encompasses all
With eternally still presence
As a multidimensional aspect of the Cosmic Dance
The universe is forever emergent and convergent
For the Cosmic Dance is Eternal

ENTRANCE TO THE GARDEN

Open French doors, framing the empty wicker chair
That overlooks the garden…
Threshold experience elucidated by use of
Space, symmetry, unity, movement and
Some prominent elements of form
A place or inner state of being
That is a liminal zone, neither here 'nor there
The entrance, a threshold space
Between being inside and being outside
Typically symbolic of a turning point
A change in consciousness
An experience where one appears to be still
Yet paradoxically there is great activity happening
On the inner level of one's being
And as a result one experiences
A transformation
From "here" to "there"
A literal transformation
Or perhaps on a metaphysical level…
Dusk, twilight, the moments between waking and sleep
Are liminal zones…
Threshold space and experience
Is why I am "seemingly" forever at the entrance to the garden…

MYSTIC PHILOSOPHER

With a toss
The coin
Of chance,
The Universal
Geometrical configuration
Of energy patterns
Was revealed to us
Centuries ago
Years upon hundreds of years
You, a Mystic Philosopher
Of the exotic far East
I a Western resident
A journalist, an admirer of
Your philosophical brilliance
And literary artistry...

With an insatiable hunger
I devoured your each and every
Word,
Food for my soul...

A potential energetic pattern
Became mysteriously hidden,
A possible future lifetime to be...

I wondered then,
Had you ever read my articles about you?
Did you know of me?

Your books were known by many
You wrote of Truth, Spirituality, Compassion,
Metaphysics and Mysticism
As a journalist I mostly
Wrote of you
Your life, your teachings,
Your poetic artistry,
The depth that
Your creative genius touched the soul...
Of Love, Truth,
A wisdom beyond the complete explanation of
The written word...

A soul moved into the sound of Silence
By the poetic, philosophical power of your word...
Having met initially this way
Within your books, your poetry
And my journal articles,
Somehow
Soul touched Soul...

And now
Centuries later
Our paths converged, by coincidence,
In a discussion on
Philosophical Anthropology,

Now years have passed
And our discussions
Still inspire
And we have ventured

To the point
Of co-creating
A written verse,
An adventure parable
Of a spiritual journey
Into unfolding expanded
Spiritual awareness,
Initiation passages, and
Compassion…

Time and Space have inter-woven our Souls.
Reincarnations that
Poetically
Journey the masterpiece
That only the Divine could so
Wondrously
Design

ANGUISH

The stopping of anguish
Emerges from
The Truth of anguish as
Birth, ageing, dying, grief,
Lamentation, sorrow, tribulation,
Despair, and not getting what one wants
Grasping after material shape,
Feeling, perception, habitual tendencies
And consciousness...
Grasping after material shapes,
Is composed of Earth, Fire, Water, Air
The uprising of anguish
When one experiences sensory impingement
Annoyance, or painful feelings
Stopping anguish
Is accomplished by
Letting go of desire and attachment
To be the point at which one
Can effectively stop the experience
Of anguish
By desirelessness and detachment
By means of perfect intuitive wisdom
The internal and external elements
Really do not belong to the Self
Everything is impermanent
And thus the mind rejoices
Pleased and composed...
Experience the four elements with
Equanimity, with insight

That lends itself to non-attachment
Transcend the Earth element and experiences
Be not hostile or agitated
Under any circumstances
Remember the Divine One
Firmly establish the skill
To remain unmoved
Expand one's vision large enough
To be all inclusive
A vision of Truth that includes
All qualities
Enables one to see reality
As it truly is
Thereby releasing one from anguish
In order to establish the skill of
Equanimity, if nothing belongs to Self
Then there is no reason for anguish
Or grief over loss
Delighted by the awareness of Truth
One has reason to rejoice

AFFLICTION

Affliction
One essential aspect
Of Divine Love
A necessary component
Of Divine Love
Affliction, something deeper
And greater than suffering
Affliction takes possession
Of the Soul
With slavery
Physical suffering
Is inseparable from affliction
Yet, affliction is not
Just physical suffering
But encompasses more
The uprooting of a life
Is an affliction that can reduce one
To the equivalent of death
Social degradation
The afflicted lose all sense
Of compassion
Affliction is the great enigma
Of human life
Affliction is a
Necessary component of
Divine Love, As in friendship
Meeting and separation
Both contain some good
Similarly

In Divine Love
There is infinite nearness and
Infinite distance
Lovers, friends
Are desirous of
Becoming one
And that their union
Would not diminish
Even if great distance
Were between them
Though painful, separation is good
Because it is Love
The Divine One can never
Be perfectly present to
Embodied, physical Humanity
The Divine can be almost perfectly absent
From us in extreme affliction
As a result, joy and suffering
Are two equally precious gifts
And parallel one's Being
Infinitely close to, or distant from
The Divine
The universe in which humanity lives
Is the "distance" created by
Divine Love
Even in infinite distance
The pure effect of Divine Love
Triumphs over infinite separation
The Divine provides a Grace
That penetrates to the very centre
And illuminates all being

So that one is able to cross the Great Ocean
Affliction, the infinite distance
Agony beyond all other
And thus it is the marvel of Love
Affliction occurs by chance
And Humanity's only choice is to
Keep or not keep one's eyes
Turned toward the Divine

PHILOSOPHICAL ANTHROPOLOGY

What is the nature
of Human Nature?
Emergence surreal...
From linear, mundane existence
into a free, creative, inspirational flow
of our transcendental spirit
A direct encounter
with Absolute being
simultaneously within
yet beyond...
Illumination
where the Divine
the Mystical
embraces the Human,
Yearning deeply,
Reaching far...
Being
the Self...
from within the centre
of our heart
where the soul
comes into embrace
with its own
timelessness

MYSTICAL EXPERIENCE

Is the pivotal point
That moves one on
From the divided self
To the holistic self
The culmination of spirituality
The divided self
An inner awareness of chaos
Inner storm
The struggle between
Two souls within
Weakness of will
Versus higher life
Distress is experienced
In the process of
Such an inner struggle
Eventually the inner struggle
Of the divided self
Culminates in an emergence
Into inner unity and peace
The most salient features
Of this inner unity are
Heightened feelings, powers of action, and
New insights
Especially through experiences
Designated as mystical
One surpasses the inner storm
Of the troubled, divided self
And enters into the lasting, ecstatic
Unity of freedom and peace

THEOPHANY

Mystical
Spiritual experience
Of communication directly
With the Divine,
New awareness of Divine
Omniscience and Omnipotence
Innocent yet suffering
Never lose hope
Of ever seeing happiness again
The Divine is always close

Theophany
Direct discourse with
The Divine
Restores faith, trust
The human intellect is limited

In understanding
Acknowledge Divine omniscience
Realize Divine wisdom understands
Completely one's suffering
Journey on
Come to know the Divine more completely

Remember the strength of Divine power
Omnipotence,
Through faith hope is restored
Remember in the heart of the tempest
While in the depths of despair

That suffering is temporary
Eventually happiness will be experienced once again

Learning is progress
From Anthropocentric to
Theocentric
Understand that the Divine One
Is in the centre
See one's Self
As a small unit
Within a larger, yet
Divine plan
Realize that everything
Cannot happen for one's benefit
Alone
Eventually Divine Justice
Will reign supreme

THE INNER VOICE

If one
Is
Merely projecting
One's ego
Then
It is impossible
To even hear
The Inner Voice

When the ego
Is transcended
One becomes
Aligned with
Truth
And the Inner Voice
Becomes
Crystal
Clear

HEALING WITH CRYSTALS

Ultimately
You are Super-consciousness
Dwell in
And act from
This way of
Being
And then you will
Heal perfectly
With quartz crystals
Or with anything,
Esoterically
Crystals are vibrating
Units of energy, subtle
Attuned to the cosmic force
Essence
Crystal energy essence
Wondrously
Affects related vibrations
On the physical level
To re-establish harmony
And thereby ease suffering
Dynamic healing with
The loving help of
The healer's soul
Positive overcomes negative
And healing results
Health, balance
An even flow of energy
Intuitive interaction
Between healer, wounded being,

And the crystal,
Amethyst, rose quartz, sacred
Clear quartz crystal
Ancient Atlantis
With advanced beings
Who "walked in the light"
Healing temples of marble
Wherein was a huge circular room
In the centre a table
Made of metallic alloy,
Containing silver, ground crystal dust
And copper,
The table supported by a pyramid
Made of crystal,
Around the circumference of the room
Were cubicles used as healing chambers
Composed of walls made of crystals
Those "afflicted" were placed in cubicles

Energized by the appropriate rays
Accelerating their rate of vibration
The ceiling of the Healing Temple
Domed and composed of interlocking crystals
In varying colours
Patterns formed of ancient symbols
When the light shone through
It was soothing
Yet awesome…

LOVE AND FREEDOM
IN RELATION TO NON-VIOLENCE

Pursuit of the benevolence of humankind
As a means toward achievement of non-violence
One begins the journey inwardly

By the process of inward vision
Spiritual insight is enkindled
As one hears the Inner Voice

However it is
Through the observance of outward, or
Worldly activities that one must
Continue the journey
Responsiveness to the Inner Voice
By means of right action
Is the fulfilment of the journey

Every act, purified in Truth
And in harmony with the principles
Of non-violence
Total harmony of thought, word, and deed
Actively and consciously in service of Love

Where Love is not present, violence is present
Follow intuition, inspired feeling and intention
Love, as is Truth, are images of the Divine One
With a greater emphasis on the heart
Than the head
Love is pure, simple, and serene
Resulting in an easy communion with non-violence

Love is the law of our Being
Love is significant as an essential
Component of non-violence
The force of Love is
The only practical means of destroying
Disharmony between persons
Wonderful change can be achieved by means of
The power of Love

Freedom goes deep into the pattern of non-violence
Freedom plays an essential part
Freedom is irrelevant without non-violence

Pursue one's own good in one's way
Mindful of the goodness of one and all
Non-violence channelled through the exercise
Of freedom,
Ensures broadness of vision

And an expansion of one's outlook
To think of what we ought to be
Rather than who we are
Is the greatest contribution of freedom
To humanity
Freedom and non-violence, together linked
Will manifest from the two
Benevolence
The greatest of all human benefit

WHO DIES?

With compassion
For the eternal soul
One discovers
That there is
No need for lamentation
In relation to death

Ultimately
Every "body" dies
And yet
The Soul is
Eternal

With conscious
Self-realization
There is no death
Wear the body lightly
Then there is only
Compassion
For the eternality
Of the Soul

WHO AM I?

"I" can be understood
From a limited perspective
As this physical
Body, mind, and emotions;
Then naturally what follows
Is material compassion
When one has compassion
Only for that
Which is material
Then there is
Great lamentation
At the loss of
The physical body
At the time of death
One experiences
Despair and affliction
From a complete perspective
One can understand "Who am I"?
As realization of the real Self
Transcendent and eternal in nature
With such self realization
One does not identify the "I"
With the physical body alone
Rather the "I am"
Is defined as an
Eternal Soul...
When one identifies
As eternal Spirit-Soul
Then at the time of death
The eternal Soul simply

Changes the body
Transmigrating to another body,
Either material of spiritual
The eternal Soul
Is a fragmental portion
Of the Divine One…
When the sky
Is reflected in the water
The reflections represent
Both the sun and the moon
And the stars also
The stars are like
Living entities
The eternal Souls, the many individuals
That take on a particular
Physical body for a time…
The sun and moon is analogous
To the Divine One
Be steady in understanding the "I"
As eternal Soul
Realize the difference
Between matter, ever-changing
And Soul, Eternal
The Eternal Soul, the "I"
Has no death
The experience of
Edgelessness of being, the Soul
Is experienced as the Divine itself
Light, unfiltered, unqualified by false
Identification
Make room in our hearts
For the true "I am"

DEWDROP

Honey'd with clear, golden and lavender,
Spring's blossom bringing forth new beginning,
Dawn awakens and glistens
In luminous flux; Oh artist of birth
Your Universal light of incandescent glow
Dances within my body, mind
Heart and Soul; Oh auspicious dewdrop,
Like a pendant of crystal chandelier,
Shaped like a tiny pear…
I see you at play upon flowers of spring,
I behold you everywhere, even in morning's
Drop of dew
Oh artist Divine, absolute in purity and
Perfection
Behold me in your infinitely vast
Creation
Hear my heart's deepest desire,
And answer me with your
Song of Love

POWER OF TRANSFORMATION

Spiritual by nature are we...
Humble beings of humanity
Dynamic, ever evolving
One is both Being and Becoming
And does simultaneously manifest
The static and dynamic
Aspects of reality
The inmost aspect, the centre of stillness
Sanctions and supports the eternal dimension
Of creative nature, the two dimensions
Inseparable, integrating
With a view to transformation
To intensify and advance, perhaps
Bridge the gap between what is
And what can be, the distant ideal
Into creation of present human reality
The force of Super-consciousness,
The power of transformation

SELF-TRANSCENDENCE

A total offering to the Supreme within
Self-transcendence demands a self-surrender
Perceived as at once infinite and eternal,
Simultaneously an endless creative flow
All at once individual, universal, and transcendental
One and many, many and One and
Many in One; Inner discoveries,
Steps on the upward journey
To the realization of a totally observant
And infinitely participatory creative consciousness
Accept all the various states of consciousness
As aspects of integral Self-awareness

EGO

Reason is only
A part of Truth
What is visible
Is only our ego
Behind which is
Concealed
The cosmic individual
It is the intuitive
Mental intelligence
That helps with
Luminous seeing

JOURNEY

The universe and the individual
Are constant and inseparable
Companions
On the journey
Of self-transcendence
A tangled story
Of ignorance and troubled desire
Into the summits of Spirit's
And Soul's ascent
To the Eternal Truth
Of Super-consciousness

COMPASSION

Suffering awakens desire for freedom and
Feelings of compassion for others
Through such life experience
Learn what suffering is
And come to understand
The sufferings of others,
Then life goes on…
With growing insight
And understanding
Capacity to feel compassion
For one another
Broadens, deepens
Rooted in understanding
Finally our hearts
Are warm with Love

POWER

Freedom is power,
Power
Follows thought...
Though the qualities
Of matter and energy
Are indestructible
There is no creation, no destruction
The total energy of the universe
Remains the same
Nothing is created or destroyed
There is only appearance and disappearance
When a thing is "produced"
It is transition from
Potential Being to Actual Being...
The purpose, the power
Is to present experience of
The relative world
And lead consciousness
From relativity to Absolute
Liberation,
Freedom

MYSTICISM

Wondrous pilgrimage of the Soul
Beginning at the soles of the feet
Then inspirationally
Through the alchemy of Love,
Transcending onward
To the top of the head
And into the depths of the heart,
Real Bliss can only come when
We return to our true home
Everlasting happiness,
When our Soul rejoins its source
In this world
Soul is sighing endlessly
For the Divine, Eternal One

UNITY

Under seemingly great diversity
Flow unity and harmony
The essence of all is the same
The same Transcendental Reality
Underlies this world of appearances
All are waves of the same ocean

DIVINE MELODY

Nearer to us than
Our hands and feet
Nearer to us than
Our own breath
Not to be found
In temples, mountain caves
Or forest fastnesses
Not hiding somewhere
Beyond the horizon,
Such joy on realizing
The Divine Melody
In our own heart,
Loving Grace of the One
That can connect our consciousness
With the Immanent Power
And take us to the place
Where the divine Melody descends

PEACE AND HARMONY

The fabric of our life
Is woven with mingled yarns
Of good and evil,
In this world, this body
We cannot but experience
Alternate joy and sorrow,
Pleasure and pain, health and disease,
Riches and poverty, honour and shame
There is no unmixed pleasure or pain alone
If world-oriented we obtain only transient happiness
Lasting bliss…only when we orient toward the Divine
Only when we transcend insipid pleasures
Of the senses, only then peace and harmony come,
The nectar of real joy…
Remember we did not come here
To make a fortune, to climb the social tree,
Or to become famous, such things are
Treasures of the world that do not endure,
Transcend the domain of matter and mind
Untie the intertwined knot of mind and Soul
Realize the inner Self and
Glow with spiritual radiance

THE ETERNAL ONE

The Eternal is One,
The way to the Eternal
Is also One
There is no second way,
This ancient wisdom
Is the timeless path,
We free ourselves to
Unite with the Supreme Being
And thus discover Eternal Bliss

SPIRITUAL NECTAR

As soon as our concentration
Is complete upon the spiritual eye,
The direction of our concentration within,
We will hear the Divine Melody
That was always there,
It comes from the highest;
The most delicious nectar is
Constantly descending within us
From above,
If we concentrate our full attention
At the point where this
Heavenly nectar is flowing
We enjoy the Bliss Divine

DIVINE REALIZATION

Not to be found
In deserts or forests,
On mountaintops or
In the depths of the seas...
Only to be found
Within our own selves,
By the secret of uniting
The Soul with the Divine Music,
The Stream of Life,
Which is transcendental,
Beyond the senses, time and space,
Our spoken or written word
Is the means,
The unspoken, unwritten Word
Is the end,
When once we have the key
We can discern the Unity in diversity,
The pathway to liberation

THE FIRST TOUCHSTONE
So long as the mind
And the senses are extrovert
They can never experience
Spiritual Bliss,
The loss of desire
For sense pleasure
Is the first touchstone a
Blossom of Spirituality

EVERYTHING TURNS DIVINE

Live in this world but be not of it,
Like a lotus,
Rise above and even
Flower from the muddy waters,
Live with Absolute Perspective;
Everything that happens reveals
The Divine, Eternal One;
Then "all" have one taste,
And the Eternal is the same
In life's bitter moments
And sweet pleasures,
Realize that life's joys are
Little more than pain in disguise,
And therefore seek the Eternal

ADORATION

Enraptured desire as
I melt
In such silence
That awakens affection
With your strong, warm eyes,
You see deep into
My very essence
I cherish the beauty I see
Reflected in you
Love dances all around
Affections fascinate
Enraptured by the moment when
Our eyes found one another...
Charmed by seductive yearning,
Affection so sweet...
Heart does melt
In our abode of Love

PROSPERITY

True prosperity
Is absolute
Without desire
Everlasting

SPIRIT

Of spirit bold
Gallantry shines,
Resolution manifests
A firmness of confidence
Fearlessness casts light anew
Upon emerging Self-reliance,
Confidence gives birth to
A fortitude, a chivalry,
Known only to those
With the virtue and intrepidity
To venture free…

GODDESS
(for Leah-Rose)

Goddess, embodying an
Other-worldliness,
Radiant inspiration creates
The halo that does sanctify
The very earth
Upon which you stand
Heavenly-minded yet humble
You enshrine beauty,
Holiness, spontaneous devotion,
Your gentle faith
So sacred and venerable,
Does edify your presence
With Grace

BENEVOLENCE

The milk of human kindness
Flows freely
With kind-heartedness
Beneficence brings forth
Charity, the foundation for
Acts of kindness
Have one's heart in
The right place,
Bring forth responsive
Interaction, compassion
That creates gracious
Community, enter
Into the feelings of others
And render generous
Bountiful living

ENDEARMENT

Enticing caress
Wins my heart
Affections
Serenade my Soul
Enrapture, enamour
Charm and fascinate
Oh sweet seduction

WONDER

Lost in wonder, you
Bewilder me
With your miraculous
Love, ornate and
Flamboyant, adorn me
Like a spangle of
Precious jewel
Set ablaze, highlight
Every aspect of me
With the wonder of you

ASCENT

Escalade, uprise
"Esprit Fort,"
Oracle of shining light
Venerable luminary
Ascend like a
Skylark free
Sagacious and
Open-minded
The fire of genius,
Meditation
Is the prism
Phosphorescent, luminous
With ardent spirit
Soaring

ANGEL
(for Jared)

The fire of genius
Solidity, sapience,
Universal expanse is
The compass of your thoughts
Clear sighted, you see far
Wondrous angel, you descend
From the vast heavens
To journey as a demigod on Earth
Into my life, as child Divine,
Wise as a serpent, mysterious and
Ever sagacious, acute in perception
With rationality, depth,
Perspicacious and judicious
Your wisdom is piercing
Refined and worthy of
Reverence, your obsequious command
Is most distinctive and inspirational

LUMINARY
(for Brandon)

Splendour of the flaming hill-top
You illuminate with incandescent
Brightness; blazing star,
You bring good fortune,
Dreams come true as
Luminescence dispels
Shadows of the palpable obscure,
With effervescent sensitiveness,
You reside at the zenith
Of the topmost summit,
You are radiant beyond
The greatest expanse,
And yet aspire to surmount
The cerulean, azure skies

SWEETNESS

You are sweet as honey
Saccharine with nectar,
Sweet as a nut
You dulcify my moments,
The nectar of my Soul,
The honeysuckle of my garden,
Like manna, you are the molasses
Of my bread and render my days
Sweet, you are my ambrosia
Exquisite, luscious, delectable,
You are my lavender balm
Elegant and flowing,
You are my peace

SERENE

Peace of mind
Embraces well-being
Conciliatory, moderate, enduring,
My heart is set at ease
Like patience on a monument
I am comforted by your love
Satisfied and serene
Contentedness reveals
All is set right,
I am snug with the
Cozy comfort of you

INTEGRITY

You are a treasure
A masterpiece,
One in a thousand
A jewel, superlative,
Your rare wizardry
Excels within and
Transcends beyond
Humble humanity,
Your presence
Is perpetually beneficial,
Splendidly sterling,
Your super-excellence is
Most precious and
Exquisite, selflessly giving
For the benefit of one and all

RHAPSODY

Ecstasy inspires
Within dreaming
Inspiration conceives
A rhapsody
Takes flight of fancy,
Imagined fantastical legend
Invents an original vision
That the dreamer and
The rhapsodist has already
Given loose to the fancy
Of romance

IN HIGH FEATHER

From light-hearted vivacity
Emerges a beauty that
Blossoms from within,
Take heart and inspirit
Lightsome merriment
Free and easy
Joyousness enlivens
A buoyant and debonair
Brightness of being

HEALING WORDS

Rose colored, auspicious,
Of good omen and reassuring,
Your healing words bring hope
And foster a reverie
Of aspirations, dreams;
You embolden my Soul
As you speak to me
With light heart...I am...
Sanguine with buoyancy,
Uplifted in spirit
In propitious promise
I cheerily rejoice
With vivacious dalliance

RIVERSONG

Imponderable, pneumatoscopic
Gentle, soft, flowing waters
Metaphysical, poetic dance
Bless and sanctify
With your sacred
Celestial song,
Reverential and heavenly
You grace me with
Blissful theophany

FLOWER

Peculiar in your
Blossoming eccentricity
Omnifarious and diversified
Unconventional, exceptional
Fantastic and rare
With beauty in full bloom
The total expression of
Unique array

THE DOVE

The spirit of Truth
Elegantly flies
A sanctifying flight
Of blessed at-one-ment,
Hallowed and wise
You are adrift
In the skies
As a sacred, divine,
Heavenly celestial
With wings outstretched
Omnipresent and omniscient,
All-merciful dove
You bring peace and infinite power

FOR A TRANSFIGURED MOMENT

For a transfigured moment
Her spirit was transparent
Beyond the narrow prison
Of her customary perception
Suddenly she discovered her Self
In a world
With no limiting doctrines
No pretensions
Where love was less
Intent on self
And Self was more solitous
Than ever dreamed
But soon she returned to "reality"
The more she tried to analyze
Whether healing miracles could happen,
Had happened, the more she saw again
Her deep-rooted indoctrination that
Everyone was supposed to bear

MYSTICAL FORCE

Mystical force
Flows into
The most darkened
Corners of life
And illumines,
Even as the lighted
Window does
Cast its glow
Across the earth

COINCIDENCE

An angel came down
And stirred the waters,
The waters of life,
And filled them with
Healing,
Chance is
The Divine at work
The whispering of the Eternal,
Fate is cosmic purpose
And coincidence is Divine Order,
Live with an endless horizon
See the vastness of infinite vision

EXPOSITION OF TRUTH

A Truth which is
At the same time
Relative and Absolute;
Gossamer wings of thought
Are impressions carried
To the Source of
Inspiration

SILENCE

Silence carries
Healing, comfort and
Happiness
Discovery of the
Power within
Stirs up the spirit
Yet dwells most surely
In the calm

EDGE

Having walked the
Edge of tragedy,
Through meditation found
The secret,
Of the secret place,
Inner peace, listen
To the still small voice
Within;
Learn to still the senses
Hush certain impulses
Enfold a mystic kind of serenity
Even in circumstances that
Easily toss most of us about

ENUNCIATION

An enunciation of
The power of choice
Affirmation
Changes life
Acceptance
Affirms life
So that one's world
Becomes a new and
Different world
Within the framework
Of the world
As it is,
Toward betterment
By the touch of
Light
Progress originates
From within

SPIRITUAL HEALING

Healing is not only
Of the body
It is of the mind
And the heart
And the spirit,
Of the whole
Consciousness,
The spiritual
Light of healing
Encircles eternal life,
Let there be healing,
And know that in
Whatever happens
Far beyond our knowing
Eventually all is
For some ultimate good

DEEPER SIGNIFICANCE

The fullness of
Time has come,
There is no need
To hurry or
Be hurried,
All is in
Divine order
Even apparent
Reversals in fortune
Have some deep meaning
Which will
Unfold in good time,
Divine life encompasses
And embraces
The way of
Spiritual meaning

BLESSING

Like an ever
Winding road
You never give
A blessing
Without
Receiving
One

LOVE

As water is the lifestream
Of rejuvenation, similarly
Love is the most powerful
Of all the emotions, live the dream
Of Love; harmony, pleasure in life
Content with the present and
Enthusiastic about the future,
A prelude to creativity and
Inspiration…as if in a pleasant,
Watery dream, calm and inviting,
Nurtured by life, feeling balanced,
Satisfied and tranquil

DREAM VISION

In that brush
With Divinity
That leaves only
Endless, overwhelming
And consuming Love
An angel appears,
At a moment of
High glory, bearing a
Countenance like lightning
And garments white as snow
Composed of spiritual matter,
Made of light, goodness
And the brilliance of
Divine discourse

ENCHANTMENT

If you were not serious
If you intended to continue living,
A useful but easy life,
Then know what waits for you
Be afraid, since you will face disenchantment,
But if you will really live with
Enchantment
Then begin a long and intense
Metacognitive process, a
Deep examination of
Your life and values…
…She did change her life,
She did accept the challenges
And responsibility, She never deserted
Or neglected her children,
But her marriage eventually
Came to an end;
Celestial beings brought warning
And appropriated fear,
Not the spillway of Grace,
She came to feel they were
Watchers, guides,
She did heed the way
And lived the miracle of
Enchantment

MICHAEL

Prince of Light
Chief among the
Angel princes,
Protector of Israel
Your symbol is
The sceptre,
Lead the army
Of Divine angels in
Defeating evil
Defend us, be our safeguard
Michael, power of the Eternal
You wield such a mighty
Sword and shield,
Conduct the spirits of
The just to heaven, Angel of
Righteousness, mercy and
Sanctification
Who is as
Divine Justice

GABRIEL

Angel of the moon
Who brings the gift
Of hope, your symbol is
The lily, you are the
Angel of judgement
Presiding over all that is;
Powerful, there are times
When you visit
That you leave auspicious
Footprints behind;
Beautiful Gabriel
You are the
Messenger Divine

RAPHAEL

Angel of prayer,
Love, joy, light,
Providence and especially
Healing
Preside over every
Suffering and every affliction,
Charged to heal the Earth
You serve as a guardian, guide
Matchmaker, teacher, healer, companion,
You carry the pilgrim's staff
Gentle and affable
Ever honoured and adored

URIEL

Fire of the Divine One
Guard the way
To the tree of life,
Sharp sited angel of
The Heavens,
Gliding through
On a sunbeam, you carry
A scroll, and you are
Swift as a shooting star,
Uriel, you are radiant as
The Angel of interpretation and
Illumination

METATRON

With seventy-two mystical names
Prince of all angels, you are
The chancellor of heaven
Ruling angel of the seventh hall
The innermost, holiest sanctum,
The true abode of the Divine
Prince of the presence
Head of the celestial academy
You hold the keys of illumination
The light of discernment,
Prince of mysteries, with
Control of all the
Secret treasures of
Hidden wisdom

THE FOUR DIMENSIONS

Within the first world,
The realm that humankind
Does live in, one does
Discover the physical, material realm;
The second world is
The place of ten hosts
Of angels, presided over
By Metatron;
The world of lights is the third world;
Lights that stream
From the highest Realm Divine.
The fourth world
Is where the
Feminine and masculine
Counterparts of the Divine
Are united.
Beyond them all is the
Mystical contemplation
Of what no one can imagine,
Yet this path of contemplation
Leads always to a higher and
Higher ability to love
That all life is holy
All life is the Eternal, Divine
One, that everything we do
In this exalted state of
Contemplation constitutes an
Act of creation, an emergence of
New angels out of the Divine
Sacred in itself, and an act of
Transformation
In the material world

THE ETERNAL DIVINE COUPLE

In the highest realm
Of the transcendental world
The Eternal Divine Couple
Are at play, majestic, merciful,
Inconceivably, simultaneously
One and different, precious and
Adorable in wondrous original form,
Giving all time and attention
To their loving relationship
In Bliss Absolute, transcendent yet
Immanent within each being,
The highest manifestation of Love,
That captivates as no other can;
The Supreme realization of the Divine
Is to realize the Eternal Divine Couple
And the highest, most wondrous goal is
To reawaken our spontaneous True Love
And graciously return home,
Into the dalliance of
Eternal Love Divine…

DANCING WITH WINGS OF SILENCE

Angels live,
They live in
The Heavens,
Angels play in
The space of eternity,
In the centre of
Our hearts,
We each serve as messengers,
As angels Divine,
Touched by wings of silence,
A sense that we cannot ignore,
We enter into bliss sublime,
Our pastimes as the
Dance of angelic acts

www.ingramcontent.com/pod-product-compliance
Lightning Source LLC
Chambersburg PA
CBHW031256290426
44109CB00012B/614